Kamala Harris

A Biography of an American Vice President

Jerry Wilson

Table of Contents

Introduction 1

Chapter 1: Kamala's Childhood 3

Chapter 2: Kamala's Education 11

Chapter 3: Kamala's Career to Date 18

Chapter 4: Notable Achievements 26

Chapter 5: Kamala's Primary Political Views 33

Chapter 6: How She Came To Be The Vice President 40

Chapter 7: What Might Be Next for Kamala Harris? 47

Conclusion 55

Introduction

On January 20th, 2021, Kamala Harris made history when she was inaugurated as the first female vice president. She also became the first Asian, black woman to be made V.P. and hold the highest political office in the land, second to the presidency. While many mourned the loss of possibility when Hilary Clinton failed to become the first female president in 2016, they were given renewed reason for hope when Harris managed to cinch the spot as Joe Biden's V.P. This groundswell of enthusiasm and hope infused the democratic ticket, and Harris' victory is widely seen as a victory for all American women, particularly ambitious young girls of color and first or second-generation immigrants who see no reason not to dream big.

Kamala Harris' life encapsulates a fascinating journey, one that represents the country's growing diversity and multiculturalism, which began in earnest during the 1960s. She was born to a family for whom social justice and engagement with political causes were never seen as fringe issues but rather informed their daily life. As a young girl, she attended civil rights marches with her parents. She was the first generation of children in Oakland, California, to be bussed into white schools, an early attempt at integration within the education system. Some of these things may be hard to fathom now, but they are part of America's recent history, which is fairly easy to forget in today's world. Before she even realized it, Harris was at the forefront of this new American "experiment," which took place in the wake of the Civil Rights Movement. These formative experiences undoubtedly shaped the woman she eventually became.

So, while women are perhaps still frustrated from the fact that a woman has yet to become President, there has been plenty of reason to celebrate Kamala and her achievements. Amid a raging global pandemic and the worst economic crisis this country has seen since The Great Depression, a woman has finally ascended to the country's second-highest position of political power. Moreover, a woman of color from a mixed, culturally diverse background to boot. Her accomplishment touched many people during a deeply difficult time in American history, thus accounting for the piqued interest in her life and her backstory.

Even though Harris wrote and published several books - including her 2009 treatise on handling criminal recidivism, which is a much-lauded part of her oeuvre - surprisingly little has been shared about her life. Perhaps this is partly because she is mostly a private woman and that her name became more prominent as news of the coronavirus dominated the news cycle. Regardless, the interest in her life and upbringing has been all the rage as of late, which is, of course, unsurprising. Harris, after all, is not just a public figure, but she is a history-making one, too.

Chapter 1: Kamala's Childhood

Kamala Harris' back story reflects the nation's diverse makeup, and her childhood is emblematic of some of the major societal changes of the 1960s. Born October 20th, 1964, in Oakland, California, she was brought up in a mostly African American neighborhood in Berkeley. Her parents were socially engaged individuals who brought along their then-baby daughter on civil rights marches. Politics and the motivation for social change were never a peripheral concern for Harris and her family. Instead, it was front and center, which her childhood so vividly illustrates.

Origin Story

Perhaps the very early point of Kamala's origin story is a bit well-known at this point. But, the exact details still seem a bit murky to many. Essentially, Harris's parents were both born in 1938 and arrived in California on a scholarship. Both were determined to get the best education they possibly could to change their fate and that of their family members. To this generation, education was the most important thing, and it was an impulse that led to a whole cohort of well-educated first and second-generation immigrants. This part of the equation is hard to eliminate from Kamala's story.

It also bears mentioning that her father, Donald Harris, was inspired to study at UC Berkeley by accounts of students from universities who traveled from the Jim Crow South in the early days of the civil rights movement. Everything about Harris's drive to succeed and fight for social justice was implicit in her upbringing from the very start.

New Immigrant

Harris's mother, Shyamala, emigrated from India in the late 1950s to attend school at UC Berkeley and earn her degree in the U.S. She may not have intended to stay for long in the country, but that changed once she met the Jamaican-born Donald Harris.

Harris's parents met soon after arriving on campus. Shyamala was equally interested in the fight for equality as Donald, which led her to befriend several black students and even joined an off-campus reading group devoted to studying the overlooked work of black authors. This group is now better known as the Afro-American Association, and its members were influential activists within the emerging Black consciousness movement. While Kawanza was first being officiated as a holiday and in meeting with different Black Power and Black Nationalist leaders, Shyamala first met Donald. By all counts, both seemed perfectly matched and immediately became close.

The young students quickly became a couple and were soon married. Both became incredibly successful individuals in their own right. Shyamala carved out a renowned career for herself as a breast cancer researcher, and Donald worked to become a Stanford University economics professor. Their drive to succeed was an early marker of Kamala Harris's life, and her parents provided strong examples of what the immigrant experience could provide in America. While times were undoubtedly rough, especially in the early years as they worked to establish their careers, it was a time of burgeoning opportunity and hope.

It seemed that great things would lie in wake for both Kamala and her younger sister Maya.

Maintaining Close Ties

The Harris's, a mixed-race family who took pride in their respective backgrounds, ensured to instill in their young children a sense of attachment to their roots. For her part, Shyamala ensured that Kamala and her younger sister, Maya, held close ties to their Indian heritage and raised them with Hindu beliefs, keeping many traditions close to heart. The girls also visited the country every couple of years in an effort to instill a strong sense of identity.

Unfortunately, close ties to their heritage is one thing, but maintaining close ties as a traditional family unit was difficult, and the parents eventually divorced. Kamala was only seven years old when the parents separated due to professional opportunities that came knocking for Shyamala, and they moved to Montreal, Quebec, Canada, when she was twelve.

According to Harris's account of her parent's separation, things were pretty copacetic between the adults even during this challenging time. Her father wanted to move to take a professorship at the University of Wisconsin-Madison at the time. Shyamala felt that her abilities were not especially appreciated by her workplace. As a result, they divorced, and Harris's mother won full custody of the girls. However, it does not seem to have been an acrimonious split, and as Harris has talked about, her parents did not fight about money but rather, who would get to keep the books they owned. In the short term, the family remained in Berkeley, and Harris was bussed to a white neighborhood for school.

While Berkley provided a well-protected cocoon of sorts, and both parents received plenty of support from the local community, living there still felt deeply alienating. Shyamala faced a great deal of outright sexism in the professional sphere, not to mention racist attitudes. She strongly felt that this limited the scope of the offers made to her, and, of course, she was not wrong. Harris vividly recounts visiting her mom with her sister at the lab where she worked as a cancer researcher but was primarily relegated to clean test tubes.

When the girls couldn't visit their mom at work, they went to a daycare center run by the Twenty Third Avenue Church of God, an African American Protestant Church in Oakland. The woman that the girls felt most attached to at the center was Regina Shelton, who maintained a close bond with both sisters. Many years later, as Harris was making history, being sworn in as California's Attorney General and Senator, she used Shelton's bible for her swearing-in ceremony. Through the daycare center, Harris's deep relationship with the African American community was also cemented, as well as her involvement with political dimensions, and community organizing. So, while the girls were always well aware of their ties to the Indian community, it did not come at the expense of their social engagement with Oakland's local African American community.

But soon enough, because Shyamala was not receiving the sort of job opportunities her education and extensive research deserved, she decided to take the plunge and move to Canada, where greener pastures awaited the young family. So, it seems that the eventual move to Quebec would be for the best for herself professionally and for her family even though the girls missed their local Oakland community very much.

A Woman's Right to Education

From the very beginning, Shyamala was disenchanted with the lack of education her female Indian counterparts received. At the time, it was rare for Indian women to graduate from college, and she was somewhat of an anomaly in her community when she decided to apply to Berkeley. She had applied in secret, with no one finding out until close to the last minute. While neither she nor anyone in her family had previously traveled to the U.S., she decided to embark upon the journey alone once she received her acceptance letter. Her parents were supportive, and her father gave up a sizable chunk of his savings to help fund her first year of school. Feminist ideals were part and parcel of Harris's history early on, and she never forgot how privileged she was to have parents - and grandparents - who were willing to sacrifice so much so that their daughter could have a good education.

Early Interest in Politics

During her time in Canada, Kamala learned to converse in French and seemed to flourish in the new setting. While it was a difficult transition for the family to make, it also presented the girls with different opportunities to grow and explore new things. For one, Kamala learned to cultivate her natural political interests when she led a protest against a building owner who wouldn't allow kids in the neighborhood to play on the lawn. It seems that the early influence imparted by her parents and their commitment to civil rights left a profound impact, and she felt compelled to exercise her rights in a way that perhaps wouldn't occur to many youngsters. This is a charming scene to imagine now. It is an important note to remember in the biography of a figure like Kamala - a neighborly spat over playing on the neighborhood's property turned into a spark for a social movement. Harris's comfort in standing up for herself and others in her community was made clear from an early age.

Teen Years and Beyond

Harris stayed for a few years longer in Quebec and attended Westmount High School, where she pursued other interests outside the political realm. Dancing is an artistic pursuit she enjoyed and even founded a dance troupe with her friend. The high school is notable for being one of the most ethnically diverse schools in Canada. As for Harris, she is well remembered by her teachers and peers for being an academically strong student who was also popular and immensely well-liked. It seems that her multicultural background was a boon and allowed her to navigate the ins and outs of various ethnic groups - and the usual high school cliques - with a measure of finesse and ease.

But, those idyllic years in Quebec would soon be over, and it was time to explore college opportunities back in America. Harris elected to go to Howard University in Washington, D.C., a renowned institution also beloved for being one of the most famous HBCU - historically black colleges and universities. She devoted her studies primarily to political science and economics while also dabbling in the debate team and becoming part of the liberal arts student council. She made the most of her college years and has since spoken of her time at Howard University fondly, for giving her a much-needed sense of community while also nurturing her natural talents and helping her find a career path about which she is deeply passionate.

Her sisters in the Alpha Kappa Alpha sorority can also attest to Harris's engaging personality, and they all remember their college years fondly. Through the sorority, Harris showed her natural kinship for other women and brought them into her orbit as the young women shared their dreams and goals. Harris is also remembered for consistently talking about her childhood in Oakland as the first generation of fully integrated students, being the daughter of an Indian mother and Jamaican dad, and exploring both parents' distinct culinary traditions. But it wasn't all fun and games, and even in the sorority, the group talked about serious issues and how to campaign for their community.

After earning her B.A., she enrolled at the University of California, Hastings College of Law, to earn her J.D. So, in 1989 she moved yet again, with her eyes set on a future in politics. Although exactly how she wanted to cultivate this aspiration was not immediately clear to her.

Early Career: A Prelude to History

Kamala's first official foray into the world of politics began soon after she was admitted to the State Bar of California in 1990. Once she passed, she began working as a deputy district attorney in Alameda County. She maintained that position for several years. Eventually, her hard work paid off when she became the managing attorney of the Career Criminal Unit in San Francisco's District Attorney Office in 1998. This accomplishment was followed by another feather in her cap when she was appointed as the chief of the District Attorney's Office Neighborhood Division in 2000.

Kamala had accomplished a great deal at a fairly young age, mostly thanks to her rich childhood and the discipline afforded by her inspirational parents. Having a multicultural upbringing worked in her favor tremendously. It offered her an intuitive ability to communicate with others regardless of their backgrounds with relative ease, which cannot be said of all politicians.

Chapter 2: Kamala's Education

Born in Oakland, California, in 1964 to an Indian mother and a Jamaican father, Kamala Devi Harris created history on the 20th of January, 2021, by assuming office as the 49th Vice-President of the United States of America. By doing so, she became the first woman to be elected as the Vice-President in over 200 years of America's glorious democratic history and the first person of African-American and Indian-American descent to hold the office. With her diverse and multicultural background and as the first female Vice-President of the United States of America, she carries the weight of the hopes and dreams of a large section of the American people on her shoulders. With her academic, political, and diverse cultural experience, it is evident that she is well prepared and more than capable of rising to the challenges that the job entails, doing justice to the high expectations that are set before her. Having spent most of her childhood in Canada and vacations in Africa and India, Kamala Harris's education mostly occurred across borders before she moved back to America for her college education.

Academic Influences on Kamala's Life

Kamala Devi Harris was born to Shamayal Gopalan and Donald J Harris. Her mother was a biomedical scientist whose work on progesterone receptors stimulated and greatly advanced Breast Cancer research. Born in the Madras Province of British India, Shamayal Gopalan moved to the United States of America after gaining her bachelor's degree in Home Science from Lady Irwin College, which is part of the esteemed Delhi University. She followed up her Bachelors Education with a Master's Program at The University of California, Berkeley in Nutrition and Endocrinology, and subsequently earned her Ph.D. in 1964. Having worked as a breast cancer researcher at the University of Illinois at Urbana-Champaign, she later moved to Quebec as a researcher at the Lady Davis Institute of Medical Research and McGill University's Faculty of Medicine.

Kamala's father, Donald J Harris, is also an academic, a Jamaican-American economist who now serves as professor emeritus at Stanford University. His work mainly revolves around the economics of developing countries. He met Kamala's mother, Shamayal Gopalan, at a meeting of the Afro American Association, a student group at the University of Berkeley, and they got married in 1963.

Growing up in a household of academics had a big influence on Kamala Harris's education. After her parents' separation in 1970, she often visited her mother's home in India, getting to know her maternal family and India's diverse and colorful culture. Her visits to her mother's home were accompanied by long interactions with her maternal grandfather. As per Kamala Harris, she has been heavily influenced by her maternal grandfather, P. V. Gopalan, an Indian Civil Services officer who served as the Director of Relief Measures and Refugees in the Government of Zambia and as an advisor to the President of Zambia. He also served as the Joint Secretary to India's Government, the third-highest non-political executive rank in India. As a 5-year-old child, Kamala also spent a lot of time in the late 1960s in Lusaka, the capital of the newly independent African country, Zambia, while visiting her maternal grandfather. Her maternal grandfather's strong and progressive views on democracy, civil rights, equality, and women's rights impressed her.

Kamala's education went beyond formal schooling. By the time she graduated from school, she had already visited India, Jamaica, and Zambia multiple times. The exposure to such diverse cultures and the academic background of her parents and her near family at such a young age understandably influenced her education and childhood. In Kamala's own words, when her parents separated, "They didn't fight about the money. The only thing they fought about was who got the books." Most of her formal schooling was done in Canada in a French medium school. She later moved back to America to pursue her higher education. Her diverse background often leads people to draw comparisons between her and the former President of the United States of America, Barack Obama.

Early Education

Kamala Harris's formal education began in Berkeley. She went to kindergarten at the Thousand Oaks Elementary School, located in one of Northern Berkeley's more prosperous regions. While she lived in a region predominantly composed of the black community, the elementary school she attended was predominantly white, with over 95 percent of the students belonging to the white community. However, this changed after the integration drive carried out in Berkeley in the early 1960s saw the ratio of black students in the elementary school increase to over 40 percent. The district's expanded bus fleet allowed students from different parts of the district to be bussed to schools in different sections to promote inclusivity and reduce segregation. As part of this desegregation program, Kamala Harris bussed to the Thousand Oaks Elementary School. Although only an elementary school, the education there had a lasting impact on her. She credits her first-grade teacher, Mrs. Frances Wilson, as one of the teachers who went above and beyond and stayed in touch with her even beyond her college education. Naturally proud of its alumni, a mural featuring Kamala Harris with other female leaders and notable personalities has been created outside the school.

When Kamala Harris turned 12, her mother moved to Montreal, Quebec, Canada. Her mother, Shamayal Gopalan, accepted a research and teaching position at the Jewish General Hospital affiliated with the esteemed McGill University. Kamala and her sister Maya Harris pursued their primary education at the Formation Artistique au Cœur de l'Éducation School (The Fine Arts and Core Education School), run by the English Montreal School Board. The school is a bilingual school teaching in French and English and has built a reputation in Canada for its excellent music program. The school was located right across the road from the McGill University, which naturally made it convenient for the family.

After completing her primary education at the Fine Arts and Core Education School, Kamala Harris joined the Westmount High School in Westmount, Quebec. The same school Leonard Cohen attended and the only public high school in Quebec that offered Advanced Placement Courses. The school was initially made up of very rich Anglo-Canadians who lived in isolation from the rest of Montreal. It was part of the Protestant School Board of Montreal, which had also guaranteed the school's existence. Although being a public school, it had a better ranking than most of the private schools. However, circa 1976, there was a major change in Quebec's Anglo community due to a separatist party coming to power, which caused a mass exodus of the Anglo-Quebecers. This exodus left the school in a tight situation as many of these people controlled the economy and were incidentally based in Westmount. As the Anglo-Canadian community could no longer sustain the school, the

Protestant School Board of Montreal removed the regional restrictions in place and expanded access to the school. It gave the not-so affluent neighboring regions the opportunity of free education from a well-established and highly rated school.

From 1978 to 1981, during the period that Kamala Harris attended the school, it had a rich cultural diversity among its students, from the very rich children of Westmount to the not-so-wealthy immigrants from the neighboring regions. While this diversity initially posed many challenges, it also contributed to the well-rounded development of the children. Kamala's education at the school wasn't limited to classrooms. Her classmates recall that while Kamala was always prepared and forceful in intellectual discussions, she also participated in fashion shows, worked on the yearbook, participated in the Pep Club, and often sang while accompanying the school mascot. She was also known as a disco dancing teenager, holding her own on the stage. Kamala Harris graduated in the year 1981, and then she moved back to America for her college education.

Professional Education

Throughout her schooling, Kamala Harris, in one way or another, attended schools where a majority of students were white, from her Berkeley elementary school to her middle and high school in Quebec, Canada. However, as a teenage girl determined to have a different life experience for her college education, she decided to attend a Historically Black College or University (HBCU). In 1982, Kamala joined the Howard University in Washington D.C. The university was then considered the most prestigious HBCU, often referred to as the "Black Harvard". She majored in Political Science and Economics and became a social activist, participating in various protests against apartheid in South Africa. Like in her previous schools, a major portion of her time in Howard was spent learning outside of the classroom. She interned as a mailroom clerk for the Senator of California, headed the economics society, and was part of the Alpha Kappa Alpha sorority.

The education at Howard University had a major influence on her. Reminiscing her time at Howard University, Kamala Harris once wrote, "That was the beauty of Howard. Every signal told students that we could be anything — that we were young, gifted, and black, and we shouldn't let anything get in the way of our success." The years spent at Howard University were extremely formative and played a major role in directing her ambitions, goals, and interests.

After graduating from Howard University in 1986, Kamala Harris moved to California, the state where she started her schooling, to attend the University of California's Hastings College of Law and worked to become a Lawyer through its Legal Education Opportunity Program (LEOP). During her time at UC Hastings, she headed the university chapter on Black Law Students Association and graduated as a Juris Doctor in 1989. However, the educational journey of a lawyer does not end with graduation. Being a lawyer is a lifelong learning profession, the first test of which is the bar examination. The examination is essentially the gateway to crossing the bar in the courtroom that separates the general spectators from the courtroom officials. Kamala Harris was admitted to the California Bar in June of 1990 and was hired as a district attorney in Alameda County, California. Her story from here onwards is history in the making.

Born to parents who were extremely capable and renowned researchers naturally impacted Kamala Harris's education and outlook. Coming from a culturally diverse background, Kamala had the opportunity of interacting with her relatives both in India and Jamaica, and as a young child also spent a lot of time in Zambia, where she was strongly influenced by her maternal grandfather's strong and progressive views on democracy, civil rights, and gender equality. Her education went full circle. From attending her kindergarten in California, then primary and high school in Canada, she returned to California to attend one of the most prestigious HBCU, Howard University. She later moved to UC Hastings to become a lawyer. A major portion of Kamala's education was outside the classroom as she participated and led debate teams, protested for social rights, and headed economic and law societies. She describes her mother as her role model, often crediting her for teaching her resilience. She once said that her mother was the greatest source of inspiration in her life.

Chapter 3: Kamala's Career to Date

From a district attorney to an attorney general, then a senator, and finally vice president, Kamala Harris's career is a defining path we can inspect to see how she rose through the ranks. It's certainly intriguing to see how well she was doing before becoming the United State's first female vice president.

First Unofficial Job

Her mother was a breast cancer researcher in the biochemical endocrinology section in the NIH, and Harris would clean pipettes in her laboratory, usually after school and on weekends. Growing up in such a science-friendly environment made her deeply appreciate what her mother and other scientists were doing. Her interest was always social and public improvement by becoming a lawyer, but she always viewed science as a noble pursuit.

Harris and Willie Brown

Harris's first official position, which later catapulted her into other positions, was the deputy district attorney in Alameda County, California. She was praised as a strong prosecutor with formidable potential. Willie Brown, the California Assembly Speaker, appointed her to two different positions; Unemployment Insurance Appeals Board and then California Medical Assistance Commission. The relationship between Harris and Willie Brown was the center of a lot of criticism. Many people in the Capitol described her as his girlfriend, suggesting that he exercised his power to get her to these higher appointments.

Harris spent 6 months in the Unemployment Insurance Appeals Board as Brown's direct appointee, which she then resigned from. During those 6 months, she also worked in the California Medical Assistance Commission since it was not considered a full-time post. The commission was responsible for negotiating contracts to reduce Medi-Cal costs. Brown's seat in the Unemployment Insurance Appeals Board was replaced by Sunny Mojonnier, a San Diego Republican.

According to the Los Angeles Times, Kamala Harris and Willie Brown were in a relationship traced back to 1994. Kamala Harris was 29-years-old when she began her work in Alameda County District Attorney's Office, while Willie was 60. A major critique that surfaced was that Harris was having an affair with a married man but was refuted since Brown had been separated from his wife for a while by the time he dated Harris. Overall, this didn't look good in the media who were reporting heavily on Californian political leaders' corruption at the time. Kamala worked hard to defend her work on the commission, saying that the commission's work was very important and that the workload was heavy.

Assistant District Attorney and Proposition 21

In 1998, Kamala Harris was named the assistant district attorney by the district attorney of San Francisco. She led a team of 5 attorneys as the chief of the Career Criminal Division, which specialized in the prosecution of habitual offenders, in addition to homicide, robbery, and sexual assault cases. In 2000, tension was visible between Harris and the district attorney's assistant, Darrel Salomon, over the newly passed Proposition 21. This proposition provided prosecutors the option of trying underage defendants, under 18, in Superior Court.

Juvenile courts were the usual courts that handled these cases, but this proposition opened the door for prosecutors to take it to another court, which used to be an exclusive option for judges of the case. While both Salomon and Harris were against Proposition 21, tensions arose due to the direction of the media inquiries. After she was reassigned, Harris quit and filed a complaint. It worked in Harris's favor as she was appointed in San Francisco City Hall in August 2000. Working for city attorney Louise Renne gave her the momentum for her D.A. campaign. Harris was responsible for running the Family and Children's Services, specializing in child abuse cases. Renne was a strong endorser of Harris's campaign.

District Attorney of San Francisco

Harris prepared to run against Hallinan and Bill Fazio for the chair of District Attorney of San Francisco. Compared to her two opponents, Harris's name didn't resonate with the public as strong as theirs. Yet, Harris managed to convince the Central Committee not to endorse Hallinan. The general election was between Harris and Hallinan in the runoff round. Harris had 33% of the pre-general-election vote, while Hallinan received 37%.

Harris displayed her stern position and pledged to never go after the death penalty, in addition to only persecuting 3rd-time offenders. Harris had strong backing for her campaign, led by a joint effort from former mayor Willie Brown, who strongly backed Harris ever since their paths crossed, Senator Dianne Feinstein, writer Aaron Mcgruder, and even actor Chris Rock. During the runoff round, Harris focused on undermining Hallinan's inaptitude, specifically his technological incompetence, focusing on his incredibly low conviction rate of 52% for serious crimes, contrasting it with the average statewide percentages above 80%.

Harris mentioned gun violence in poor neighborhoods and spotlighted Bayview and Tenderloin, blaming Hallinan for his inclination to accept plea bargains easily in domestic violence cases. Harris's aggressive campaign managed to snatch her a win against the odds, making her the first person of color to be elected DA of San Francisco. In her second term, Harris's win easily came as she was unopposed.

Moving Against Non-Violent Crimes

Environmental crimes were heavenly damaging the city's poor communities, which is why Harris spearheaded an environmental crimes unit in 2005. She assigned two staff attorneys and an investigator to manage the unit that focused on investigating claims of environmental damage to the city, like the dumping of printer inks and unhygienic restaurants.

Harris went after San Francisco's supervisor Ed Jew for the unlawful tampering of legal documents to retain his supervisor position. Jew was against 9 felonies presented by Harris, the most prominent ones of which were lying under oath and providing fake documents to prove that he lived in a Sunset District home. Jew pleaded guilty on other unrelated federal grounds, such as mail fraud and extortion. He later pleaded guilty to falsifying his address, which was done in order to run for the supervisor position in the fourth district.

Even though Harris's office got over 1,900 convictions for marijuana cases, which was a substantially higher rate than Hallinan, fewer defendants were sentenced to state prison for such cases. Low-level marijuana offenses were almost not targeted by Harris's office, especially with a non-jail-time policy for possession cases. Even after Harris left the District Attorney's office, her successor expunged the offenses going back to 1975.

Gun-Related Crimes

During the time Harris was the Attorney General of San Francisco, she had to fight a huge backlog of homicide and gun-related cases. The murder rate per capita in San Francisco was significantly more than in other cities and the national average. Harris managed to secure a very high conviction rate for homicide and felony gun violations between 2004 and 2006.

Harris was cracking down heavily on gun-related crimes as she constantly pushed for higher bails for gun-related violence. Harris's anti-gun position was far from being subtle, and she even mentioned that outsiders could take the opportunity of San Francisco's loopholes to get away with their crimes. She created a special gun crime unit that directly worked to reduce the chance of defendants getting bail without bonds. She advocated for a 90-day minimum for possession of guns, in addition to treating cases of assault with guns involved as felonies. The unit was highly focused on landing maximum penalties for such crimes.

Hate Crimes

One of Harris's most popular violent crimes units was the Hate Crimes Unit, which handled hate crimes on school grounds involving LGBT children. The Gwen Araujo Justice for Victims act was a byproduct of Harris's effort to initiate collaborative efforts between hundreds of prosecutors and officials in a 2-day conference. The act resulted from the murder of a Latina transgender teenager by two adult men; her name was Gwen Araujo. Harris was focused on helping the jury overcome bias, prejudices, and public opinions when deciding such trials.

Harris's Position on Death Penalty

Harris was a strong advocate for removing the death penalty from the penal system. She mentioned that a penalty of life imprisonment without parole possibilities saves more money than the death penalty. Harris's campaign was highly vocal about her anti-death-penalty leanings, which was put to the test in 2004. The murder of an SFPD officer sparked political pressure from U.S. senators Dianne Feinstein, Barbara Boxer, and S.F. Police Officers Association, trying to force Harris to reverse her position on the death penalty, but she still held it.

Harris Running for the Attorney General of California

Two years prior to the Attorney General election, Harris announced her intention to run. The main condition she mentioned for running for office was if Jerry Brown, the current Attorney General, decided not to go for reelection. Brown didn't run for the Attorney General office and focused his effort on the governor position, which helped Harris get the support she needed from known California Democrats during the election. During the primaries, she was heavily endorsed by House Speaker Nancy Pelosi, Senator Dianne Feinstein, Dolores Huerta, mayor of LA Antonio Villaraigosa, and other prominent members of the Democratic Party.

Republican district attorney Steve Cooley was Harris's main opponent in the general election. The election took around 23 days, with Harris coming out on top after a rather long time tallying up mail-ins and provisional ballots. She was the first woman in history to hold the position of Attorney General of California. A few years later, Harris publicly announced that she would run for reelection, which many prominent media outlets endorsed. She won the race against Republican Ronald Gold.

The U.S. Senate Election

Senator Barbara Boxer announced that she wouldn't run in 2016, after 20 years of serving as a U.S. Senator. Harris followed with an announcement a week later that she would be running for the Senate seat. In 2016, the California Senate election used a new and different format, where the party wouldn't consider the two top candidates in the primaries. Harris won 78% of the Democratic Party's vote, which helped back her with enough financial support. Harris managed to steamroll the general election against Loretta Sanchez, the Democratic congresswoman. With major endorsements from the President and the vice president, Harris achieved enough momentum to capture 60% of the vote.

Senate Judiciary Committee

In January of 2018, Harris replaced Al Franken after he resigned from the Senate Judiciary Committee. In the same month, she questioned the Homeland Security Secretary for his favorable bias towards Norwegian immigrants. In May, the same person was questioned again by Harris about the family separation policy, a controversial policy that separated illegal immigrant children from their families. Harris was very vocal about being against this policy and was the first senator asking the DHS chief to step down from his position. During her time as a senator, Harris was a member of several committees, including Homeland Security and Governmental Affairs, Budget, Intelligence, and Judiciary subcommittees.

The Vice President of the United States

Initially, Harris was planning to be in the presidential race of 2020 and was considered a top contender for the Democratic Party, but she withdrew in December 2019.

She announced her vice-presidential campaign on April 17, 2020. After being elected the Vice President of the United States, Harris resigned from her Senate seat on January 18, 2021. Walter Mondale, a former senate-turned-VP, mentioned that the vice-presidential office is "both a legislative and executive branch," especially with the sharply divided ratio of democrats and republicans in the Senate.

Chapter 4: Notable Achievements

With her career soaring high, Kamala Harris has bagged many achievements to date. While some are controversial and raise several questions about her morals, others are testament to her beliefs and principles. Among several achievements and milestones that Harris has covered to date, we will be discussing the most notable ones in this chapter.

Her Feats as an Attorney General

She was the lead attorney general of California and was applauded for her work during her early years. As DA in San Francisco, Harris floated the Back on Track program, which allowed drug offenders to complete schooling to avoid jail time. She believed that everyone deserves a second chance. Her stand on mitigating the law surrounding the third felony also made headlines. According to Harris, the DA's office would only lock up an individual with a serious or violent crime under the third felony rule.

Her role as a DA and attorney general was not easy. Harris went through several ups and downs that involved questioning her decisions, opening investigations, and criticizing her pro-establishment decisions. In some cases, she was also questioned for falsely defending police officers and conducting an improper prosecutorial misconduct investigation. Harris's decisions and appeals around the death penalty laws also raised a lot of questions.

Later, her new criminal justice reform took a new turn as she introduced several policies for the betterment of the country;

this made her a strong proponent and put her in a new light. Some of the policies revolved around removing solitary confinement, abolishing private prisons, legalizing marijuana, and eliminating cash bail. Her support for equal marriage rights and actions against human trafficking cases and for-profit institutions are noteworthy, too.

Her contribution to bringing billions of dollars in settlement and relief to homeowners cannot be ignored. The $25-billion settlement with major mortgage institutions covered legal protection and helped homeowners in turmoil and individuals who lost homes.

Recently, the mayhem surrounding several African American murder cases involving Breonna Taylor and George Floyd led her to co-sponsor the Justice in Police Act by the Senate. Another bill formed in 2020 that declared lynching to be a federal crime was also co-sponsored by Harris. Furthermore, several ethnic and racial groups faced disparities in 2020 due to the advent of the COVID-19 pandemic. Harris realized the need to form a task force and monitor the issue with scrutiny.

She Holds Numerous "Firsts" to Her Name

As you now know, Harris was the first African American and first woman to become an Attorney General of California. Prior to that, she was also the first black woman to hold San Francisco's District Attorney's position. She wanted to do things differently and had a vivid perspective that not everyone supported; this also pushed her into several controversies and debates. In her early years, her work and actions made her a progressive prosecutor, something she always aspired to be.

Ever since becoming the U.S. Senator in 2016, she has been in the limelight for various reasons. Her role as a member of the Intelligence and Homeland Security committee is well-known. Her distinct questioning style and varied perspective have always garnered attention during Senate Hearings. She also received mixed but heavy reactions during Supreme Court Justice Brett Kavanaugh's interrogation. One of the critics was the former U.S. President, Donald Trump.

Along with Republican Mike Lee, Harris created legislation in 2019 to look into the green card caps across the country. Countries like China and India can greatly benefit from this as the backlog makes it difficult for those countries' citizens to migrate.

Being an avid activist, Harris has also sought after climatic and civil rights issues, not only in the United States but also in other countries. For instance, she has proclaimed her desire to work with China on climate change and any other common interests they share. She has also shown concern for the country's Uighur minority, facing human rights issues and abuse. The complex relationship between the two countries has made the situation a bit convoluted.

Harris is also known as the first Indian American and Black woman to get a presidential ticket. As she says, "I may be the first of many, but I will not be the last," thereby inspiring women and children across the globe.

An Active Member of the Alpha Kappa Alpha Sorority

The Alpha Kappa Alpha sorority has been a highly coveted group created at Howard University since 1908. This sorority group is the first Black Greek Letter Organization that protects the values of women. Harris attended the university in 1986 and became an active member of the HBCU. This group typically consists of the Divine Nine, which involves nine Black sororities and fraternities. She joined this sorority group because she was offered the freedom of being herself and owning her skin color. In a way, people believe that her participation in this community had a major influence on her ticket to becoming vice president.

Created *OpenJustice*, an Online Database Platform

This online platform was made available in 2015 for common people to access the database to achieve complete transparency. The data collected from thousands of law and criminal enforcement agencies was made available on this platform. The ability to compare different entities also allowed the general public to dig deeper and unravel the truth. For example, anyone could openly compare the Los Angeles Police Department with the San Francisco Police Department. Data types, such as the annual number of arrests, deaths related to arrests, and deaths in custody, were openly available to view. Harris's strong will to change the inner system also played a major role in this feat.

A Colossal Activist

Ever since she was a child, Harris has been a colossal activist and fought for various rights. While her parents were all over Berkeley and Oakland in California fighting for civil rights (since the University of California was an active ground for activism), young Harris found her agenda as well. She was an active member of protests and has never been afraid to speak her mind.

Harris's maternal grandmother, Rajam Gopalan, was a great influence as she witnessed her being an active member of protests and fighting for women's rights. Her South Asian roots and ideals have ingrained a sense of awareness and pride that has, in a way, inspired Harris to fight for the right and dodge the wrong. Upon her mother questioning her reasoning for attending a protest, she proudly declared, "FREEDOM!"

Some of her popular campaigns and stands as an authoritative power include:

<u>Reproductive Rights</u>: Upon Justice Ruth Bader Ginsburg's demise, Harris fought for reproductive rights for women in the country. When Harris was a speaker in North Carolina, she actively stated every woman should be allowed to make decisions for her own body, defending the right to abortion and appealing the need to change laws surrounding reproductive rights.

<u>Gun Rights</u>: Harris led a presidential campaign in her early years, which was unsuccessful. However, she made some strong points and suggested actions that could curb gun violence. Apart from banning guns and weapons, she also suggested the need to conduct background checks on individuals and entities that sell more than five guns annually. Those who did not cooperate or comply with the rules could lose their license. She also proposed that the gun owner be mentally fit to use any kind of lethal weapon as it could hurt them or others. Her strong appeal on background checks for both the dealer and buyer was favored by many.

Health Care: Senator Bernie Sanders proposed eliminating private health insurance and proposed "Medicare for All" which was actively backed by Harris. With time, she kept private health insurance in place and instead focused on providing better and active health care access. Her vision was to provide health care to every resident in the country. When she stood as a nominee for the Vice-Presidential post, she backed Joe Biden's plan to make healthcare available to the public at much lower costs.

Racial Discrimination and Policing: Harris was an active participant in a protest in Washington D.C. that was held for calling out George Floyd's death in 2020. She also took time to meet Jacob Blake's family and speak with him over the phone after the unfortunate shooting event. She also demanded a complete investigation to unfold the truth and charge the officer.

As mentioned, Harris also supported the legalization of marijuana and decriminalizing it. However, her early years witnessed thousands of people being arrested for drug infractions. With this, she wished to expunge convictions of the past.

Author of Three Popular Books

Not many know this, but Harris is an author of three popular books that have become even more popular since becoming the Vice President.

Smart on Crime, 2009: Harris's years of experience as an attorney are reflected in this book. She debunks several myths related to the judiciary system and how it can be improved. While several books revolve around the rhetoric of strengthening the criminal justice system, Harris focuses on how the system can truly be changed. The false choices one makes and the necessary shifts that need to be introduced are also sensitively weaved within the book. Furthermore, she also covers the need to reduce costs and bring communities closer. In the book, she writes, "If we take a show of hands of those who would like to see more police officers on the street, mine would shoot up."

<u>The Truths We Hold, 2019</u>: In this book, Harris portrays her sense of pride and strong cultural roots that give her the courage to fight for her rights. Since her mother always feared the racial discrimination that she and her sister would face growing up, they were taught to be confident, strong, and fearless. This book was a New York Times bestseller and labeled as inspiring and uplifting from an American leader's point of view. Harris also delicately mentions the urgency to find one's truth and abide by it; this will bring people closer and help them take better control of their lives. In this book, you can read about Harris's upbringing and the ideals she followed as a child growing up.

<u>Superheroes Are Everywhere, 2019</u>: This illustrated children's book was Harris's first attempt at a different genre and portrays her love for superheroes. She puts forward an empowering thought and conveys the message of us being surrounded by superheroes. She inspires children to be heroes. This book also gained the title of New York Times Best Seller. Harris uses her childhood stories and experiences to inspire children to find their inner heroes and become better people as they grow.

She also loves cooking and has displayed her love for good food in a Glamour Interview. Harris gives all the credit to her mother, and she actively shares food ideas and recipes on her social media. She has also participated in culinary activities during a campaign.

Chapter 5: Kamala's Primary Political Views

From the moment Joe Biden chose Kamala Harris as his running mate, much was made of her supposed ultra-left bonafide. The reality is quite different, and as a politician, Harris is much more of a centrist than is popularly believed. While much has been made of her historic candidacy and current position as the first woman, first Asian, and first black woman to be vice president, there hasn't been quite the fulsome conversation around her politics, which she admittedly deserves. Not only is it important to understand her politics given her position, but Biden is currently seventy-seven years old, and the public should be clued into her viewpoints and potential policy gambits should anything happen.

Luckily, Harris has had a long career in public service and has written extensively about her politics. So, there's plenty of information out there for those who'd like to learn more about what she represents. Here are a few key points on her policies and positions that will help shed some light on how her brain operates.

Health Care

During her presidential run, long before Biden chose her as his running mate, Harris lost quite a bit of support among Democratic voters for her position on healthcare. Specifically, the idea of Medicare for all. She flip-flopped and was not very consistent. Of course, this was before the pandemic appeared on the scene in 2020, so the most potential supporters gravitated towards Bernie Sanders and Elizabeth Warren as a result. However, her lack of a clear position was not always the case.

As a Senate freshman and only beginning to get recognition in 2017, she was one of the biggest names who latched onto Bernie Sanders' single-payer bill. At the time, she noted that her conscience urged her to join the bill, and she felt that it was "the right thing to do."

However, during the democratic primaries nearly two years later, she began to backtrack. Her initial position entailed the idea of going as far as eliminating private insurance companies in favor of a government-run system. The backlash from the general public and other candidates on the ticket selling themselves as moderates was swift. So, she backtracked. But even that move proved to be quite deadly, as more supporters left her. Her poll numbers tumbled quickly since her core beliefs on the matter were difficult to pinpoint at the time, and liberals and moderates within the Democratic Party were split.

Since then, she's been attempting to find a middle ground. The idea was a plan that gave Americans the ability to choose whether they wanted a private health insurance plan or a public one. But again, this centrist position did not curry favor with too many people, and Harris has since avoided making another policy proposal on the health care front. At the same time, she has not shied away from stating that the current system only serves to create glaring socio-economic discrepancies, particularly among people of color. She has also become more vocal about the necessity of the government intervening to offer the American people help, especially in light of the pandemic, which most democratic candidates can agree on now. However, Harris has been very quiet about setting down specific policy points since becoming V.P. and is letting Biden's cabinet picks lead the way.

Consumer Protection

One of Harris's earliest "wins" in her political career came when she was still California's attorney general. She aggressively sought to change consumer protection laws and played a major role in securing a staggering twenty-five-billion-dollar settlement for homeowners in her home state from big mortgage firms. It is one of the biggest accomplishments anyone has achieved against the predatory loan sharks and housing bubble that devastated the country in 2008. The foreclosure crisis hit millions of Americans very hard, and California was no exception. Her advocacy on behalf of homeowners cemented her status as a fierce protector for consumers, and she continued taking on many cases during her time as attorney general. As the top law enforcement official in her state, she fought hard against predatory leaders and worked to protect people being hounded by student debt. She also has taken a famously tough position on online consumer privacy issues and has undertaken some of the harshest legislative positions against tech companies.

The Second Amendment

Gun control will always be one of the most controversial topics in the country. Every time politicians - especially those on the left ideologically - try to make some legislative changes or even comment on it publicly; it inevitably opens up a can of worms. It's one of the most complicated issues in contemporary American life. While there is popular support for gun control, it's been hard to substantially discuss in Congress - despite the number of mass shootings that have rocked the country. Harris has supported a ban on assault weapons and stated that she believes that the sale of high-capacity magazines should likewise be eliminated. As Attorney General, she introduced legislation to seize illegally owned firearms, which resulted in more than twelve hundred guns collected. So, her stance on guns is fairly tough, and she hasn't budged on this one.

She has continued to campaign for gun safety laws in the country, beginning with advocating for universal background checks and renewing the assault weapon ban, which only occurred on the George W. Bush administration. On the campaign trail, Harris famously said that if she were President, she would sign an executive order mandating background checks for firearm dealers and anyone who sells more than five guns a year. Unlike some other politicians who have strong arguments for gun control, she has not made gun owners the sole focus of her proposed policy amendments. Instead, she has focused on gun manufacturers and how they make guns widely available. She has also campaigned to close a loophole that allows known domestic abusers to purchase guns, which is a big issue and has led to many instances of violence.

Harris has also famously come out against a popular proposal from conservatives to arm teachers in schools to prevent mass shootings, stating that this could make the problem far worse and lead to more mass violence instances.

Criminal Justice Reform

Kamala Harris has made a career of speaking out on necessary criminal justice reform and has pursued several legislative policies on the issue of recidivism. She has made her thoughts known in a book that she published early in her career and has spoken about the importance of funneling money into federally provided resources to help people move past a stint in jail. She has never made the argument for defunding the police, nor has she advocated for such a stance in the wake of the racial reckoning of 2020. But, she has made her frustrations with the police system known, particularly as they pertain to George Floyd and Breonna Taylor's brutal deaths and how law enforcement officials - particularly in the latter case - have yet to be charged.

Harris' positions as Attorney General regarding crime have been criticized by her more progressive opponents, who feel that she did not do enough to help people who committed crimes due to economic hardship, mental health issues, etc. Some feel she may have contributed to the police forces' militarization in minority neighborhoods, so her policies have come under a great deal of scrutiny.

At the same time - and especially most recently - she has taken part in open discussions about the "over-funding" of the police in certain cities at the expense of valuable social services that have only served to increase crime and violence. Her position on the role of policing, recidivism, and the criminal justice system has been rather nuanced, and she has changed slightly since her previous centrist political views on the matter.

Climate Change

Another major issue these days is climate change and the necessary steps the government needs to take to lessen the fissures caused by the crisis. Harris has stated that she is squarely on the side of the Green New Deal and wants to build a clean economy that can help create jobs. During her presidential campaign, she unveiled a plan that looked to cull public and private funding to help build infrastructure, create more clean energy opportunities, and instate so-called climate resilience measures. Given that her state is one of the hardest hit by the climate crisis, it makes sense that she understands the urgency. Her plan has even called for net-zero carbon emissions by 2045, and she has stated that a carbon-neutral electricity sector could be set up by 2030.

Of course, much of the drive behind these initiatives was also due to Trump's disregard for things like the Paris Agreement, which many democrats felt was an egregious mistake. Harris stated that if she were elected President, she would like for the United States to rejoin the Paris Agreement, to underscore the seriousness of the climate change issue and take part in major diplomatic missions again with the E.U. - something that changed under Trump.

During her campaigning for the presidential nomination, she also announced that she would hold corporations accountable for any damage inflicted upon the environment. She has continued to hold firm to that position, especially since the terrible wildfires have ravaged much of California, and tornado after tornado, and other forms of extreme weather have wreaked havoc across the nation.

Minimum Wage and Progressive Economic Measures

Harris joined other progressives on the minimum wage issue and believes it should be raised to fifteen dollars an hour. Like her colleague Bernie Sanders, she advocated for a livable wage and has expressed dismay that the minimum wage has not been raised in more than a decade. She also voiced her support for equal pay between men and women and having federally mandated paid family and sick leave. This issue has driven many American families to the brink of bankruptcy.

Specifically, Harris was lauded for her proposals to invest more money into black-owned businesses and historically black colleges and universities, noting the economic discrepancies that cut across racial lines. Being an HBCU graduate herself, she knows what a vital organism they are and that they can lift whole generations of young people, both morally and economically. She sees investment in HBCUs as a necessary conduit to ensuring greater economic prosperity that will help solve systemic racism issues.

When it comes to taxes, Harris advocates for more progressive reforms to help America's middle class. The plan would give middle-class families up to three thousand dollars a year for single people or six thousand for married couples. The credit would be available to couples making less than one hundred thousand a year - or singles earning half that amount. It is meant to lift people out of poverty, which many families have fallen into in the past few decades due to rising inflation, stagnant wages, and concurrent economic crises - the 2020 pandemic that has followed the 2008 crisis has not helped matters.

There is so much to understanding Kamala Harris' political viewpoints, all of which cannot be covered here. Suffice it to say, there is a bit of nuance: while she is certainly more on the progressive side, she has also taken a hardline on certain matters that have caused her to lose favor with people to her left. For example, while she pushed for programs to help people find jobs instead of putting them in prison, she's also helped keep people in prison even after being proven innocent. Her track record as district attorney and Attorney General is complicated. Some would argue that this does not convey wishy-washiness on her part, as opposed to a willingness to slightly alter her positions over time and after studying all the facts. In the present political climate, she is less ideological than many of her counterparts on either side of the aisle.

Chapter 6: How She Came To Be The Vice President

Harris's journey from prosecutor to Vice President is extremely interesting. As mentioned earlier, she has had a fair share of ups and downs that have made her the person she is today.

Presidential Candidate

In 2019, Harris embarked on her political journey and set her bid for the presidency. She initially began her campaign with the slogan "Kamala Harris for the People". When she led the campaign, several questions surrounding Harris's eligibility to become a President or V.P. arose. While some claimed that she did not have an "American" ethnicity, others stated that she did not meet the requirements of being a U.S. citizen.

During the Democratic Debate, Harris questioned frontrunner Joe Biden about his record on race. The former Vice President was questioned about racial slur comments when surrounded by segregationists a few years ago. Harris also accused him of opposing busing in America in the past. In his defense, Biden justified his opposition for the system and not for the act of busing. He also cross-questioned Ms. Harris's career and doubted her stance as a prosecutor.

Harris continued to justify the need of having a Black person, and a Black woman at that, within the system and not just outside. She made a case for the strong need of having a woman of color inside the system who could closely monitor the decisions being made.

Even though she attracted the attention of thousands, her campaign failed due to a lack of funds. She could not raise funds after her first rally, which led to pulling out of the race. Harris also failed to keep black voters at her side, which further faltered her campaigns. Even though she promised to provide, several issues forced her to back out right before the first voting session was supposed to occur.

Harris's contribution and public service to her nation were reflected in her campaigns. Even though her presidential campaign was unsuccessful, it sure gained a lot of attention, which later helped her gather funding from people in Hollywood. These factors, along with the multiple statewide campaigns, helped Biden and Harris prior to voting sessions.

Becoming Joe Biden's Pick

Initially, rumors surrounding Biden joining the presidential race were scarce. He announced his presidential candidacy just a few days later. On-air debates and ribbing between Harris and Biden were a frequent sight and all over the news.

It was just within a brief period of 1 year that they turned into allies. Biden's campaign promise involved choosing and appointing a woman for the position of the Vice President. He chose Kamala Harris as his running partner, making her the first Black woman to be chosen as a nominee for this prestigious position.

John Adams held the first spot as the V.P. nominee in Biden's party. However, Biden's promise to elect a woman as his Vice President opened up opportunities for several ladies in the political arena. Some of the notable names included Gov. Gretchen Whitmer, Sen. Amy Klobuchar, former ambassador

Susan Rice, Sen. Tammy Duckworth, Rep. Karen Bass, and Sen. Elizabeth Warren. These women collectively bowed out and declared that the prestigious position should be given to a woman of color.

With Harris's strong governing powers, ability to make hard calls, and preparedness, Biden was ready to work with Harris from day one and make a difference. Biden promised Harris that all decisions would be taken in front of her and that she would not be barred from any procedure followed in the White House. It was one of the appeals that Harris considered when accepting the position offered by President Biden. Harris also considered Biden's position as a V.P. when he assisted former President Barack Obama for eight years. She believed that no one else could reflect on the position and summarize the expectations than those who had been in a similar position in the past.

It also stems from Biden's statement when he gave an interview on *The Late Show with Stephen Colbert* in 2015. He stated that even though V.P.'s do not have inherent power, your capability and relationship with the President can give you multiple opportunities to make wise decisions and make a difference. Several occasions like this demonstrated Biden's desire to have a close friend as his Vice President and someone he could trust. Like he had Obama's back, he wanted a V.P. who would stand by him.

On August 11, 2020, Harris decided to join Biden's campaign and accepted his invitation to stand as his Vice President.

Oath as a Vice President

Upon receiving the victory news, she was seen beaming and speaking the precious words, "While I may be the first woman in this office, I won't be the last. Because every little girl watching tonight sees that this is a country of possibilities." Kamala Harris swore in as the Vice President on Jan 20, 2021, and she expressed her gratitude to her mother in the victory speech.

Biden could also not contain his excitement as he stood at the Capitol and addressed the country, saying "Here we stand, 108 years ago at another inaugural, thousands of protesters tried to block brave women marching for the right to vote — and today, we marked the swearing-in of the first woman in American history elected to national office: Vice President Kamala Harris. Don't tell me things can't change!"

Her empathic mindset and ability to handle delicate situations are two essential assets that every V.P. must possess. Many consider Biden to have taken a wise decision and recognized Harris's true potential. Her former chief of staff, Nathan Barankin, also praises Harris for her preparedness and ability to juggle critical situations in her favor; this was when she served as the California Attorney General and a U.S. Senator. He further added that Harris possesses this special talent of thinking without considering herself as an individual with a high rank. She uses her empathetic mind and heart to consider others' viewpoints, which ultimately helps her arrive at a sane decision.

This can be easily reflected in the multibillion-dollar settlement case with banks that made mortgage frauds and put homeowners in trouble. Other attorney generals were focused on the size and type of settlement, whereas Harris truly dug deeper and considered the homeowners' perspective. How the homeowners would be affected, the amount of money they lost, the value of their job and children's schooling, debt, and several other factors were considered by Harris, which eventually helped them renegotiate the settlement. This mindset, Barankin added, was one of the major possessions that put Harris in this high-profile position today, something she truly deserves.

Popular Democratic strategist Jessica Byrd also had a say when Harris was nominated for the position of V.P. She hopes and expects Harris to be on the front line and make crucial decisions instead of attending to the laborious chores that a V.P. is supposed to do. She adds that the office should be smart enough to use her brains and talent to tell powerful stories and push the nation towards progress.

Steps She Took After Becoming V.P.

Just like any other Vice President, Harris is standing by the President's side in the initial stages and helping him prepare remarks and sign orders. Even though this is how most V.P.s behave in front of cameras, Biden and Harris seem to be faring and prioritizing several critical issues off camera and away from the public eye. In an interview with NPR, she stated that she and Biden have, so far, collectively made decisions and have been standing in the same room. They hope to continue this pattern in the future. As Biden promised, Harris is seen in every meeting, standing close by the President and helping him sign important documents.

Harris is known to take one step at a time and refers to her approach as "nervous optimism". Being a woman of color and many "firsts", she has all eyes on her. Her position is complicated as the expectations are outsized, even more, because of her racial and cultural heritage. Since every V.P. is allotted with a set of policy areas, the nation awaits the decision that will define Harris's role. Like Biden was given the stimulus package's responsibility and foreign policies during his time as a VP, Harris is expected to have and share equally important responsibilities.

This political arrangement also portrays a stark contrast with the former setting, where Vice President Mike Pence was barely in the picture as he was constantly overshadowed by former President Donald Trump.

The initial hand-in-hand approach by Biden and Harris is set to clear economic ramifications and control the pandemic. They are also looking into reforms of climate change and racial justice.

Harris's work has not been entirely successful during her first attempt either. News of a $1.9 trillion proposal did not sit well with a few Democratic senators mainly based in West Virginia and Arizona. There is also this faint debate about Harris's political experience and that she is too young compared to the President. Unlike Vice Presidents Dick Cheney and Joe Biden, who were older than their Presidents and therefore had more experience, Harris may have some conflict with Biden. It brings her more challenges to handle and numerous questions she must answer. However, her experience as a Senator and active member of the Judiciary, Budget, and Intelligence and Homeland Security may help her assist the President.

Today, she is labeled as "A Vice President like no other". Her barrier-breaking role in the office is instilled as an inspiration for many women and children who can now consider the United States a country of possibilities. Her achievement is not only historical but also an inspiration to the country. All eyes are on her and President Biden, and the United States residents cannot wait to see what they will be doing next. There are many things to undo, several crucial decisions to take, and numerous questions to answer.

Chapter 7: What Might Be Next for Kamala Harris?

Vice President Kamala Devi Harris has come a long way, all the way from a disco dancing teenager of Westmount High School to becoming the Vice President of the most powerful nation on earth. Coming a long way is probably an understatement. Although by being elected as the first female Vice President in the history of the United States of America, Harris has written history. The story of Harris has only just begun. The Vice-President's office opens and presents an extraordinary opportunity for improving the lives of millions and millions of people. As the Vice President of the USA, there are various challenges that she needs to overcome and promises that she must fulfill. What might be next for Kamala Harris? There are endless possibilities, from another vice presidency term to a full-out presidency campaign, the stage is set.

Kamala Harris' Term as Vice-President

Kamala Harris' term as Vice-President of the United States of America has just begun. With the United States President, Biden, promising that Harris as Vice President will be the "Last voice in the room", a lot of responsibility falls on her shoulders. With many promises made to the American citizens, the next few years for Harris are well mapped out. Here are a few things that Harris will be focusing on as the Vice President.

Focusing on Urgent Needs

In an interview with CNN, President Biden stated that Vice President Harris would focus on whatever urgent need he would be unable to focus directly on. He also added that, unlike Ex-Vice President Al Gore who focused mainly on environmental work, Vice President Harris would hold diverse responsibilities and take over urgent matters. She would be playing a major role in the Senate as she holds the tie-breaking vote, given that the Senate is split 50-50 between the democrats and the republicans. Having served as the Vice-President in the Obama-Biden administration, President Biden understands what the Vice President's job entails. During his term as Vice-President, Joe Biden had an important say in the legislatures and decision-making process, one that he intends to offer to Vice President Harris.

An Advocate for Change

Many activists expect Harris to lead the charge and be an advocate for change. Her assumption of the Vice President's office in itself has left a mark in history, and given her past advocating for social causes from her college days, social activists around the country are counting on her to lead the fight for racial justice where it intersects with policy. Activists expect Harris to help fight against the COVID pandemic that has wreaked havoc in the country, its economic ramifications, and the effect it has had on the communities of color.

Job Creation for the Masses

Before endorsing President Biden's campaign, Harris ran her own 2020 presidential campaign, and job creation was always at the forefront of her efforts, even as a senator. As part of the Biden-Harris Administration, Harris plans to create millions of jobs. This goal is at the center of the economic plan unveiled to help the country recover from the impact of the COVID pandemic. However, given the uncertain global economy, job creation at such a level would not be a walk in the park. It will require a large amount of planning and relentless effort to realize.

Affordable Healthcare

President Biden believes in The Patient Protection and Affordable Care Act of 2010, also known as Obamacare. It was an act that was proposed during the Obama-Biden administration and aimed at providing affordable healthcare to all by lowering the costs for those who can't afford it. Although Obamacare is still active, a major clause was abolished in 2019 during the Trump administration. Although Harris has always been an ardent supporter of affordable healthcare for all, as a senator, she supported the Medicare for All bill that Senator Bernie Sanders proposed. However, her focus has now shifted to Obamacare. Despite its various advantages, many doctors oppose the Obamacare act because a significant number of people that enlist fail to meet their monthly premiums, causing them to lose the benefits after 90 days. Pushing the Obamacare act forward and towards widespread acceptance is likely to be an area that Vice President Harris will support President Biden on throughout their term.

Women's Rights

During her career as an attorney and a senator, Vice President Harris has spoken out on women's rights and implored the nation to address the issue. According to her, women's rights encompass various other issues like the economy, national security, healthcare, education, criminal justice reform, and climate change. During the presidential debates, she raised the issue of women's access to reproductive healthcare, despite its controversial nature in America. An ardent and vocal supporter of women's rights, especially their right to abortions, women's right is bound to be a focus in her term as Vice President. During her presidential campaign, she also announced her plan to end the backlog of rape kits. She proposed to make investments of up to 1 billion dollars to allow and assist all the states in clearing their backlog over 4 years.

Climate Change

The first major decision made by the Biden-Harris Administration was to recommit to the Paris Climate Change Act, clearly demonstrating their commitment to the cause. While the United States of America was initially a part of the Paris Climate Act, its participation was withdrawn by the Trump Administration around fear of job losses of 2.5 million jobs.

Harris has always been an ardent supporter of environmental protection policies and supports the Green New Deal to build a clean economy that also creates jobs. Talking about climate change, she once tweeted, "The climate crisis is an existential threat that demands bold action. My climate plan will take on powerful interests and build a clean economy, create millions of jobs, and guarantee every person's right to breathe clean air and drink clean water." Her plan revolves around the investment of 10 trillion dollars through public and private funding to build an environmentally friendly economy with net-zero carbon emissions by 2045. Her presidential campaign promised the rejoining of the Paris Climate Act, one that was promptly met. But the road from here onwards only gets tougher. Environment-friendly technologies are expensive to adopt and are often met with a lot of lobbying. Working towards a carbon-neutral economy is no small task and is likely to keep Harris occupied for the rest of her term.

Citizenship Bill

Over 11 million undocumented people are living in the USA. After being elected as Vice President, Harris publicly promised by posting on Twitter that while her priority would be to save lives from the unprecedented coronavirus, next in line would be to send Congress a bill with a roadmap for addressing citizenship concerns of 11 million undocumented migrants. The "Dreamers Act" is meant for the immigrants that qualify for the *Development, Relief, and Education for the Immigrant Minor Act*, or the DREAM Act. The DREAM act intends to provide underage undocumented immigrants in the USA the opportunity to be educated, work, and live in America without the constant fear of deportation.

Gun Control

Gun Control has always been a controversial topic in the history of the United States. It has always been difficult to develop a flaw-free method that prevents the misuse of guns without violating the people's right to possess firearms. Over the years, various incidents have been witnessed across the United States that have sparked debate. Harris has always maintained a strong stance on gun control. While campaigning for her presidency, she stated that she would enact multiple executive orders on gun control, including those that would restrict the ability of those convicted of domestic violence to possess firearms, universal background checks, banning the import of assault weapons, and revoking licenses of gun manufacturers that break the law. After assuming the role of Vice President, Harris has called on Congress and urged the Senate to act on gun control legislation citing that President Biden is prepared to sign.

However, gun control reform legislation is likely to be met with a lot of opposition from the Senate and the public. It is one of the reasons such reforms have been hard to enact. However, cleverly penned legislations that can find a workaround to the problem will keep guns out of the wrong hands. Gun control is another issue that is likely to be one of her focus topics during and after her Vice-Presidency.

While Vice President Harris will be spending the next four years executing her duties and responsibilities as the Vice President of the USA and supporting President Joe Biden, she has age on her side. At 56 years of age, she has the time and opportunity to either repeat her tenure as Vice President or take over the hot seat itself.

Presidential Run

As a Junior Senator of California, Harris put forward her bid for the President of America. While she was considered a high-profile contender for the presidential seat, she withdrew her candidacy due to a lack of funds. Given that this is President Biden's first term as President, he would be eligible for another term. But considering his advanced age, he would be 83 before his next term began. Therefore, it would be unlikely that he would run for office again. Who better to fill the shoes of Joe Biden than his deputy Harris? Experts believe that Joe Biden might already be prepping Harris to be the next President while future-proofing the democrats. Former First Lady Michelle Obama stated, "Vice President Harris has already been the 'first' many times in her career. This is a woman who knows what she's doing." Furthermore, President Biden understands the responsibilities of a Vice President and knows what it takes to make it to the top of the pedestal. Harris is very likely to be a frontrunner for the next presidential elections, and even if the elections are not in her favor, she has age on her side to contend for the subsequent ones.

Author

While there have been a large number of books that have been written about Harris, she is a published and accomplished author herself. To date, Harris has authored and published three books. The first of these is a children's book titled *Superheroes are Everywhere.* In addition to this, she published her memoir, *The Truths We Hold: An American Journey*, and a third book, *Smart on Crime: A Career Prosecutors Plan to Make Us Safer*, published in 2009 just before her 2010 campaign for California Attorney General. Her books have met with good reviews and positive feedback; her memoir was rated 4 out of 5 on Goodreads and 5 out of 5 on Waterstones, which are the most popular reading communities on the internet. Their popularity has further increased after her being elected as the Vice President, with 4 out of the top ten books on Amazon being on her or by her.

Given her previous accomplishments in writing, it is likely that with her experience of the vice presidency, she would at the very least pen another book based on her learning and experience.

The next four years of Kamala Harris will undoubtedly revolve around her official duties and fulfill her promises made to the American public. But many things could follow her Vice Presidency. While she could serve another term as the Vice-President, she could well be on the way to running for the office of the President of the United States of America.

Conclusion

Kamala Harris has taken office at a pivotal moment in the country's history, and the job ahead of her and Joe Biden is immense. However, she has shown her grit, and the depth of her professional experience proves that she will be up to the task. There is a once in a century pandemic that has overtaken the world, which the administration needs to attend to, a tenuous and complicated vaccine rollout, a badly shaken economy, a broken legal system, racial strife, and more. Saying that this new decade started with a bang is a bit of an understatement.

That being said, given Harris's professional background and natural charisma, she has earned the trust of so many in both her immediate sphere and of the general public - even after a somewhat tumultuous presidential campaign. While she didn't cinch the democratic primaries, she was such a standout candidate that she was clearly the front runner as Biden's pick for vice president long before he made the official announcement. Since the inauguration, she has handled important assignments, from tracking the progress of the COVID relief bill in Congress, helping to set out the budget for that and tax credits for families, and, most recently, was tasked with overseeing the humanitarian crisis at the border. The latter mission is a particularly sensitive one given its complexity, and that diplomacy with several countries needs to be effectively implemented - especially after Trump's time in office alienated many countries in Latin America, which contributed to the crisis. Migration is one of the biggest issues today. It will only increase with the advent of climate change, hitting these particular countries especially hard, causing people to attempt the dangerous border crossing in ever greater numbers. Harris's parents were immigrants, so she understands some of the key issues migrants are concerned with. Putting her in charge of this complicated diplomatic mission makes sense.

It is still fairly early in her tenure as vice president to gauge whether her work in the Biden administration can accurately be expressed as successful. After all, they still have four years to go, and it's not clear yet whether Biden will run again for reelection with Harris or if he will step aside for another democratic candidate given his advanced age. But the administration got its start in what is perhaps the most consequential election of modern times, and Harris' tenure is already historic in many ways.

Some have said that the excitement for the new administration has been centered more on the extreme dislike people harbored for the previous President - as opposed to genuine admiration for either Biden or Harris. Perhaps there is some truth to that statement. After all, these are uniquely polarizing times, and the public has become increasingly public. But many - especially first and second-generation immigrants, women, Asian and Black Americans - watched the inauguration with wonder when they finally saw a woman hold the vice-presidential seat. Harris is an inspiration, and so many people are praying for her to succeed at the difficult tasks assigned to her.

www.ingramcontent.com/pod-product-compliance
Lightning Source LLC
LaVergne TN
LVHW021737060526
838200LV00052B/3331